TALKING PICTURES

Thoughtful strategies for visual learning for 4–7s

Fiona Moss and Stephen Pett

Contents

Introduction: using *Talking Pictures* — **2**
Ideas for visual learning with 4–7s — **3**
Teaching Christianity through pictures — **7**
Teaching Islam through pictures — **13**
Teaching Judaism through pictures — **18**
Four ways of helping lower-achieving children — **23**
Four ways of stretching higher-achieving children — **24**

Introduction: Using *Talking Pictures*

One way to engage young children in learning in RE is to use rich, evocative images. This pack provides 31 full-colour photographs of images related to **Christianity, Islam, Judaism and a wider view of spirituality**, extending beyond religious ideas. The images show contemporary religious belief and practice, including young children from Christian, Muslim and Jewish families.

The images have been chosen to be both accessible and intriguing, providing some simple information about how the religions are practised in the UK today while also encouraging a questioning response from children.

Each of the 16 *Talking Pictures* cards provides a series of questions, from simple initial questions to get children to look closely (**Beginning to find out**), through questions that build on their knowledge of the religions pictured (**Finding out more**), and extending to more open-ended, reflective questions, to get children to think more deeply (**Wondering**). Of course, the questions are just guidelines for the teacher, who should feel free to develop any particular line of questioning or respond to the comments and questions from their own pupils.

For teachers: information provides a clear, simple introduction to some of the key beliefs and practices shown in the images, in order to increase teachers' confidence when exploring them in RE. (Where teachers are unsure of the answer to a question from a child, we recommend acknowledging this and saying that you will find out the answer.)

This accompanying book includes 24 generic strategies for using images with 4–7s (many of which work well with older pupils too), linked to the images in this resource pack. There are then 13 photocopiable pages, specifically for use with the images in this pack but also exemplifying strategies that can be used more widely.

All the photographs, and the questions on the reverse of each card, are on the accompanying disc.

My most special object to do with worship? I would probably say a candle, because when I pray – at school and at church – when I am carrying the candle as an altar server, instead of closing my eyes I look at the candle really really deeply and I can see Jesus. I remember that Jesus is the light of the world and that is not going to change.

Chloe, 9, Roman Catholic

The thing I like best is being part of a community, helping each other, being peaceful together, worshipping Allah. I meet with others at the madrassah to learn to read the Qur'an and to learn about what's right and wrong.

Yahya, 10, Muslim

The best thing about being Jewish is being together with my family at special times. I love festivals, like Hanukkah where you get presents, play dreidel and light the menorah. Shabbat is the most special day in my religion. Every Friday night, me and my sister say the prayer for the candles. On Shabbat we have a rest.

Samuel, 8, Jewish

Ideas for visual learning with 4-7s

Paint-box

Ask the children to concentrate on one of the pictures, and list four colours in the picture. They should put them in order – the colour shown most often to the colour shown least often.

One way of doing this would be to ask the children to create a colour chart that the artist/designer has used, showing the colours used more as a larger block of colour.

You might get them to compare their colours with another pupil who has worked on the same – or a different – picture.

Ask the children why the artist or the designer (of a building, for example) has used these colours. What difference would it make if different colours had been used?

This is a preliminary observation strategy which gets learners thinking about the colours used and their significance.

Try this with Cards 1 and 11.

Tags

Photographs uploaded onto the internet are usually given 'tags' – these are the key words that sum up what the picture shows, so that if you were searching for lots of images of a particular subject, the search links the photographs.

Ask children to work in pairs to think of the five key words, or 'tags', that sum up what the picture shows. At the simplest level the tags will be purely descriptive (e.g. candle), but tags can be linked to mood or emotion or other concepts (e.g. calm, peaceful, prayer).

Try this with Cards 5, 8 and 14.

Ask the artist: quiz the photographer

Ask children to think about the questions they would like to ask the artist or the photographer. Try this structure:

Naming: questions about what can be seen in the picture

Understanding: questions about what is happening, where, why, etc

Imagining: questions about what it might be like for the artist/photographer or people in the picture

Puzzling: questions that they would like help exploring, where an insider's view would make it easier.

Try this with Cards 1, 13 and 14.

Look, talk and draw

Put children in fours. Give a simple picture to Pair A in the four (e.g. baptism candle, Card 5). They have to look at it together for one or two minutes before you take the picture away.

Pair A describe the picture to Pair B, and then have to stop talking while Pair B try to draw the picture. After a few minutes, you can allow Pair B to ask Pair A one question. Allow Pair B to look at the picture and talk with Pair A about how close they got to drawing it.

As children get used to this kind of activity, you can use more detailed images. You can also extend it by using Rumour Mill (below). The activity uses and develops skills such as visual memory, observation, descriptive language, co-operation and teamwork.

Try this with Cards 5 and 15.

Rumour Mill

This version of **Look, talk and draw** builds in an element of 'Chinese whispers' – or a Rumour Mill.

Have children in groups of eight this time. Pair A look at the picture for a short time, then describe it as fully as they can to Pair B. Pair B describe it to Pair C, who describe to Pair D. This of course generates confusion – it is a 'rumour mill' because the quality of description as it passes through the stages usually declines. Pair D then try to draw what Pair C described. This activity enables learners to look really carefully at what is going on in a work of art.

Try this with Cards 4 and 8.

In the gallery

Imagine that this picture is being displayed in a gallery. As a class, come up with a title for the picture. It needs to help people looking at the picture to know what it is about, but it also needs to be interesting, to make people want to look.

Imagine that two descriptions of the picture are needed – one for small people a little lower down the wall and one for tall people higher up. The description for small people needs to use small words and small sentences. The tall description can use big words and longer sentences.

Try this with Cards 5, 7 and 9.

Similarities and differences

Give children a selection of images. Ask them to sort them. You might give them an instruction first – such as which images include children and which don't, and limit it to two pairs of pictures for easy sorting.

Then ask them to see if there are any other ways of sorting the images. These might include different religions, places of worship or the home, happy/sad mood, and so on. Ask children to explain the reasons for their groupings. Explore which groupings are to do with similarities between the images and which are to do with differences.

Try this with Cards 2 and 12, 4 and 8, 5 and 7.

Questioning the images

Lay out a selection of images on some sugar paper on the tables in your classroom. Ask children to walk around and think of questions to ask about the pictures.

With younger children, you might pair them up – a writer with a non-writer; or you might have a TA or parent acting as a scribe for a group of children, to write the questions on the sheets under the images. These then allow children to see which questions have already been asked.

Collect together the question sheets and use them as the basis for your talk about the picture. Some children may be able to answer the questions already.

Try this with all the Christian cards, or two each from Christianity and Islam, for example.

Odd one out

Show the children three images, using the structure shown on p.14. In this exercise there is no single correct answer.

Children can offer different explanations as to why one or other is the odd one out. The structure on p.14 encourages children to give reasons – if A is the odd one out, it is because it has something that B and C don't have; or it doesn't have something B and C do have. Children can begin to make links and spot similarities and differences, as well as developing their ability to explain their ideas.

Try this with an image from Cards 4, 8 and 11 or 2, 10 and 12.

Bubbling speech. . . bubbling thoughts

Show the children some images, either printed out or displayed on the whiteboard. Give them some blank speech bubbles (or ask them to draw their own). Ask them to imagine what the people in the pictures might be saying. They may record these in writing or simply use the bubbles to help them think and talk themselves.

Next, give out some blank thought-bubbles. We don't always say what we are thinking, so ask the children to reflect on what the people in the pictures might be thinking.

Try this with Cards 6, 9 and 15.

Cropping or framing

Ask children to identify a key part of the image by cutting it out, or by circling it on the whiteboard. For example, which is the most important part of the image, or which part shows the heart of the story, or which part is the most interesting, the happiest, the calmest, or represents prayer or holiness or worship, and so on.

This activity can also be done by giving pairs of children a small cardboard frame and asking them to place it on the picture to show the most important part, and so on.

Try this with Cards 5, 10 and 14.

Sequencing

Give children a selection of illustrations or artworks from a story and ask them to put them in the correct order to retell the story. At the simplest level, children can be asked which picture comes first in a pair of images. For example, the aqiqah ceremony on Card 7 and the boy reading the Qur'an on Card 12. The age of the children in the image make it obvious, but you can also make the link that without the aqiqah ceremony, the boy might not go on to read the Qur'an.

Try this with Cards 7 and 12, or 2, 3 and 5.

Create a cover

Ask the children which image they would use on the cover of a book about (for example) Judaism, or celebrations, special places, happiness, love, God, peace and stories from the Bible.

What if the book is for older children? Or younger children? Ask them to draw their ideas if there is not a good enough image in the pictures you show them. What would you call the book?

With older children, you might ask them to write a 50-word blurb for the back cover, to explain what is in the book and encourage people to read it.

Try this with Cards 1–16.

And the winner is…!

Imagine that your selection of images has been entered into a competition. Ask pairs of children to choose the winner. Imagine that they are at the award ceremony and have to say a few words about the picture and why they have chosen it as the winning entry.

You might offer different competitions: e.g.

- Noisiest picture!
- Most peaceful picture
- Being a Christian in the UK today.

Ask them to find some more images online to see if they can find a better one.

Try this with Cards 1–16.

Through the keyhole!

Cover up most of an image, leaving only a small section visible. Ask children to say what they can see. Gradually reveal more of the image, allowing children to describe more and try and guess what the whole image is. Encourage them to ask questions about what might be 'through the keyhole'. Who might live in a place like this? What clues are there that this is from one particular religion?

Some electronic whiteboard software allows you to do this – otherwise, paste the image into a word processing or presentation programme and cover parts up with boxes.

Try this with Cards 5 and 9.

Drawing around

Give children half of a picture and ask them to draw what they think the other half of the picture will be like. Or give them the central part and ask them to draw what they think will be around it. Or give them a smaller part of the image – a quarter, for example. If it is a piece of artwork based on a story, give children the story too, so that they can work out what the rest of the picture might look like. They can then compare their ideas with the artist's.

This strategy works well when an image has something surprising and unexpected in the missing half, but it also helps children to look closely and to use the clues in the picture to work out what is happening.

Try this with Card 3, showing just the girl first, or 10 showing just the mother.

Jigsaw

In order to get children to look carefully at images, print and cut up a selection of pictures into two. Ask children to find and match the pairs of images, making them whole again.

Take one picture and cut it into six pieces. Ask children to make the jigsaw up.

Take two or more pictures, cut them up into six pieces each and mix them up. Ask children to disentangle the images. This might help them to learn to identify two different religions, for example.

Try this with Cards 1, or 4, 8 and 11.

It's behind you!

We get used to looking at photographs or artworks and seeing what is happening in them. It can be interesting to ask children to imagine what is going on behind the photographer, or to imagine what any characters in the picture may be looking out at. You could also ask them to extend the picture all the way around. What is happening around the scene shown?

Try this with Cards 6 and 13.

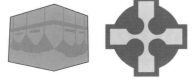  

What happens next?

Imagine if you came back to the same place on the next day, or on a Sunday, or a Friday, or on Shabbat, or at Christmas. Ask the children what might be different and why.

Try this with Cards 4 and 11.

Observations and reflections

Using the structure on p.11, children can 'wonder' around an image. Older children can write their responses, but younger children can be walked through this as an oral activity. 'We think this picture is… We noticed… We can see… We're not sure about… We want to ask about…' etc

Try this with cards 5, 7 and 10.

In the picture

Before you show the children the picture, talk them through a reflective activity, such as a guided visualisation (see p.20). Ask them to close their eyes and use their imagination as you describe walking into the picture, looking around, describing the atmosphere, mood, sounds, events, and perhaps talking to one or two of the characters.

Ask children to draw the scene you have described, then show them the artwork/photo you were describing.

How did they feel? What did they learn? How different was the drawing from the one they saw in their imagination?

Try this with Cards 8, 11 or 13.

Hot seating

After talking and learning about the ideas expressed in the photo/artwork, ask a child to take the part of a character in the image and answer the questions from the rest of the class, as if she or he were the character.

If the individual cannot answer the question, the other children can suggest answers too.

Try this with Cards 2, 6 and 9.

Taking talking pictures

The collection of images in this pack can be extended by finding suitable pictures online, but it can be very helpful if children add their own photos. Give children some digital cameras when you are next visiting a local church or mosque, for example. Set children the task to take a peaceful photo, or a busy one, or a puzzling one. Display the photos back in the classroom and talk together to come up with some questions. You might try some 'beginning to find out', 'finding out more' and 'wondering' questions.

Try this with Card 4, to find a different type of church, or a busy one.

Trading places

Now for some drama! Get your children into groups and ask them to reproduce the image, taking the place of people or characters in the photo or artwork. As they put themselves in the place of the characters – facing the right way, using the same expressions, and so on – ask them what it feels like, and what might be going on in their character's mind and body.

When they have brought the 2D image into 3D life, ask them to fast forward five minutes – what position would people be in now? Why?

Try this with Cards 6 and 9.

Teaching Christianity through pictures

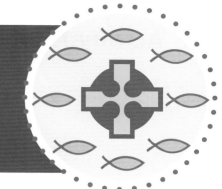

Activity 1: What really matters at Christmas?

Discuss Card 1 and share the story of the birth of Jesus. Present children either with a selection of artefacts and characters relating to Christmas or use the illustrations on p.8.

Count and learn: Ask the children to look at the items, then cover them over and see whether they can remember all the items.

What links...? Ask one child to suggest two of the items that belong together, and say why, e.g. 'camel and donkey are both used to ride on'; 'you can light the Christingle and the candle'.

In the story: Ask if the children can say what each one of these has to do with the story of the birth of Jesus at Christmas. Ask them if there are any that have nothing to do with the story. Use talk time to reinforce the story and its meaning for Christians.

Take away one by one: Discuss whether you can have Christmas without these things. Remove or cover the items one by one – each time ask whether there is still Christmas.

Most important? Invite children to say which of the items might matter most to a Christian person or might help them to remember the story of Jesus' birth.

Activity 2: Bubbling speech – bubbling thoughts

Share the two photos and discuss some of the questions on the back of Card 2. With younger children use the **Bubbling speech – bubbling thoughts** activity on p.9 as an oral discussion framework; older children can write their responses in the bubbles.

What are the two different people thinking as they read the Bible? What might they say about why they are reading the Bible if you asked them?

Activity 3: Investigating a church

Discuss with the children the parts of the church identified on the activity sheet on p.10. Explain how these parts of the church are used during a service of worship. Answer any questions the children might have. Ask them to complete the activity on p.10.

Discuss what the children imagine their classroom looks like at eight o' clock at night. Explain to them that just as with a school, sometimes a church is busy and noisy, sometimes busy but quiet and sometimes empty like in the picture on Card 4. Discuss what the church would be like on Sunday morning during a service. Who would be in the pulpit? What would be on the lectern? Where would the children be? Would they have some toys to play with? Would people be sitting, standing or kneeling?

Activity 4: Observing and reflecting about baptism

With younger children use **Observations and reflections** on p.11 as an oral discussion framework, perhaps on the whiteboard. Older children can write their responses in the bubbles, working either in pairs or as individuals.

This activity will help you to find out what the children understand about baptism and what they are interested in enquiring into further.

Activity 5: Freeze frame Easter

Share the story of Easter through film, books, small world play or creative storytelling. Once children are familiar with the story ask them to work in a group to select and create a freeze frame of the part of the story that they think is the most important. A director must arrange the scene while the actors play the parts.

Once the children have created their scene, take your magic microphone around and interview the 'director' who has arranged the scene. Why was this scene chosen? Question the 'actors' in the scene. What is their character thinking?

Once all the freeze frames have been chosen, ask the children to draw the most important part of the narrative on the TV screen on p.12. Write the children's ideas at the bottom of their TV screen.

Activity 2: Bubbling speech - bubbling thoughts

Photocopiable by purchasing institutions

Activity 3: Investigating a church

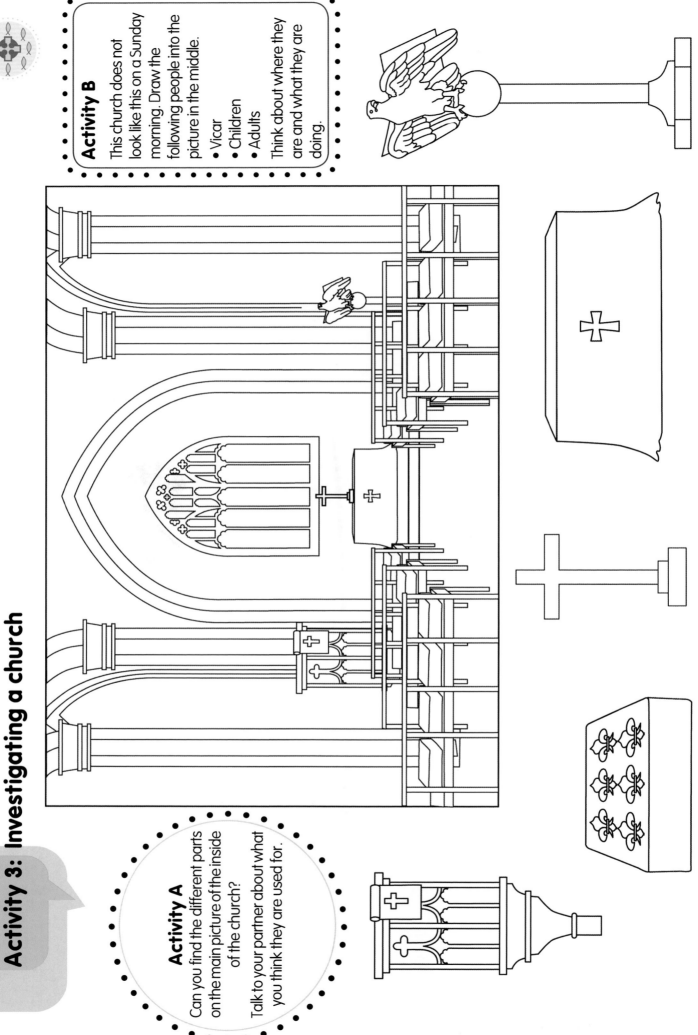

Activity A

Can you find the different parts on the main picture of the inside of the church?

Talk to your partner about what you think they are used for.

Activity 4: Observing and reflecting about baptism

Another question we have is...

We are not sure about...

It made us think about...

Our best ideas about this are...

We can see...

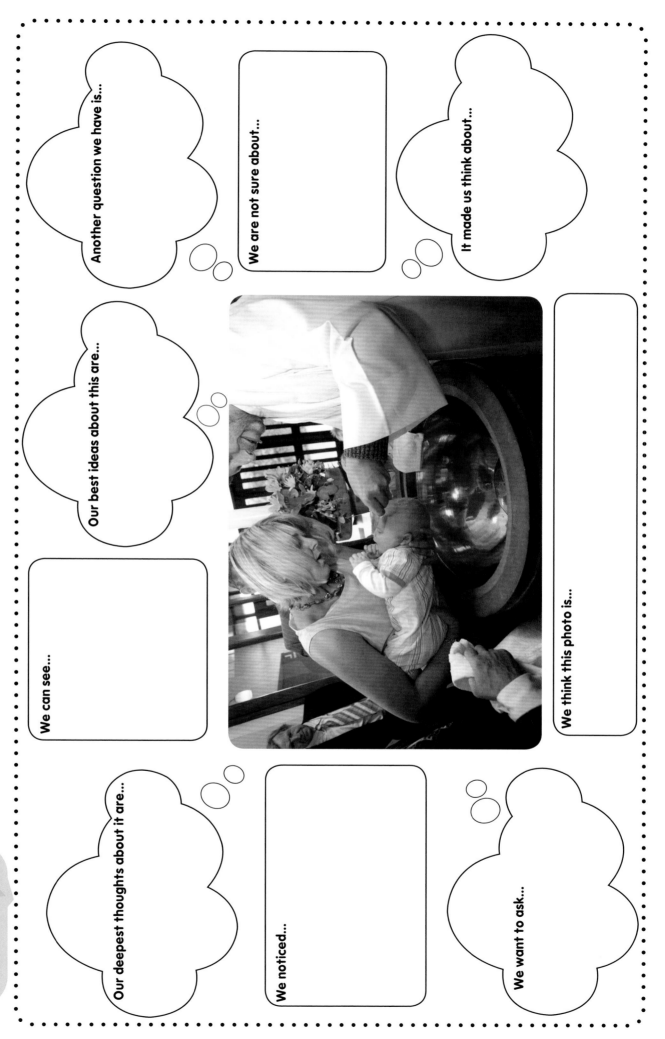

We think this photo is...

Our deepest thoughts about it are...

We noticed...

We want to ask...

Activity 5: Freeze frame Easter

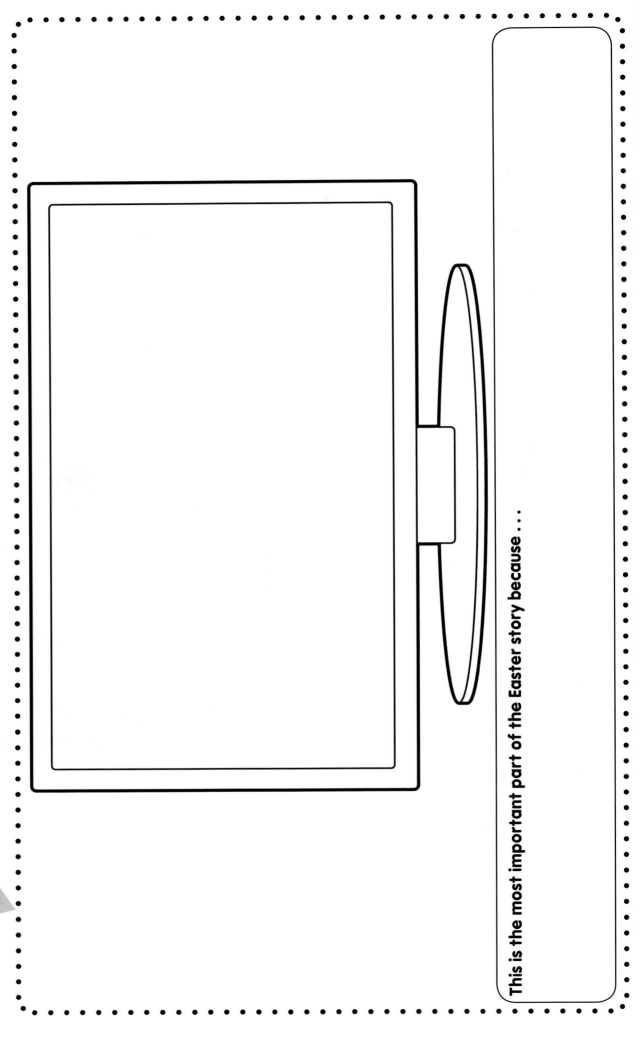

This is the most important part of the Easter story because . . .

Teaching Islam through pictures

Activity 1: Odd one out: Islam

Odd one out is a thinking skills activity which can be used to ascertain prior learning, as part of a learning activity or as an assessment for learning activity. This example could be used in each of these three contexts.

Reveal the pictures one at a time to the children. Using the activity sheet on p.14 on the interactive whiteboard, note what the children can see in each of the three pictures. Encourage them to guess at the significance of actions and artefacts in the pictures.

When all three pictures have been revealed, ask the children to:

- suggest the similarities between the different pictures
- suggest the differences between the different pictures
- decide with a talk partner which picture is the odd one out and why.

Activity 2: Investigating Eid ul Fitr

Before embarking on this activity either use Card 6 or show a short clip of a family celebrating Eid, for example, BBC Learning Zone class clips 4605 (www.bbc.co.uk/learningzone/clips). Give each group the three pictures on the activity sheet on p.15. You could supplement these with other Eid cards which are now available from major card retailers.

Get the children to think about the images and ideas on the cards by asking the questions on the activity sheet. The term Eid Mubarak means 'blessed festival'.

After they have looked carefully at the images and discussed them in groups, ask each child to create his or her own Eid card showing what the Eid festival is about. Cards might include families celebrating, praying at the mosque, putting money into a charity box or sharing food.

Activity 3: A whisper and a shout

The picture of the father whispering into the ear of his newborn child (Card 7) and the exterior of the mosque (Card 8) have something in common. You might ask children to guess what it is – the adhan is spoken in both places. It is whispered into the child's ear and also called from the minaret, calling Muslims to prayer. It shows that this call is something very important to Muslims.

Listen to a recording of the call to prayer (http://tinyurl.com/3poe2re). Ask children to think of some words to describe the sound. What do they think it might be saying?

Talk about why Muslims might use the same prayer in both places.

Use p.16 and talk with children about what they would like whispered into their ear as a baby, and what they would want to shout from the rooftops. What messages are so important that everyone should hear them?

Activity 4: Islam, art and peace

Look at the image of the inside of the mosque (Card 8). Ask the children to talk about the decoration. Note that there are no images of living creatures. There are also no images of God, as this is strictly forbidden in Islam. Instead there are beautiful patterns (the simple arch designs on the carpet and the wall, and the complex designs in the dome), together with Arabic calligraphy.

Have a look at www.patterninislamicart.com for further patterns and information.

The word 'Islam' means peace – the peace gained from submission to God. Using the activity sheet on p.17, ask children:

- to colour the pattern in peaceful colours
- to come up with their own peaceful pattern.

For some Muslims, certain colours have particular meanings, e.g. blue = infinity, green = paradise, white = purity, yellow = glory.

I can see . . .

Similarities between 1 and 2

I can see . . .

Differences between 1 and 2

The odd one out is . . .

because . . .

Similarities between 1 and 3

Similarities between 2 and 3

Differences between 1 and 3

Differences between 2 and 3

I can see . . .

Activity 2: Investigating Eid ul Fitr

Picture 1

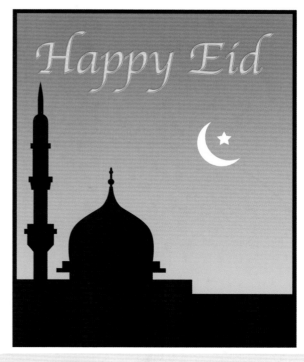

Picture 2

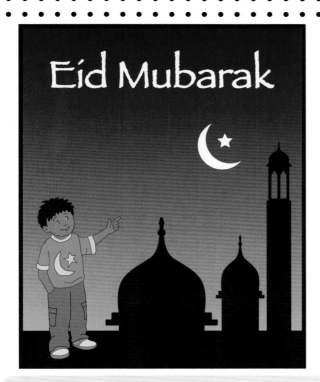

Picture 3

Investigations to follow

1 **Questions to think about**

- What do you notice about these pictures?
- What do you think is happening in Picture 1?
- What has this got to do with the festival of Eid?
- What do you think the cards celebrate?
- What clues can you see on the cards?
- What do you think Eid Mubarak means?
- What do you think it means to be blessed?
- What things might make somebody feel blessed?
- Sometimes when you buy a card some money is given to charity. Why do you think a Muslim might like to buy an Eid card which also helped people in need?

2 **Create your own card** which could be sent to a Muslim. Make sure it shows the real meaning of Eid.

Activity 3: A whisper and a shout

These are the words
I would want whispered
into my ear as a baby:

These are the words
I would shout from
the rooftops:

Colour this design in peaceful colours.

Design your own peaceful pattern.

Teaching Judaism through pictures

Activity 1: Shabbat: Doing the delightful

After showing the children Card 10 about Shabbat, spend some time learning about what is significant for Jewish people about Shabbat. Shabbat, or the Sabbath, is the highlight of the week; it is eagerly anticipated through the week and treasured afterwards. This day of rest and refreshment gives a rhythm to the lives of many Jewish people and is seen as a day to delight in.

You may want to show the children a clip, for example, BBC Learning Zone class clips 3874, 3875 or 4745 (www.bbc.co.uk/learningzone/clips).

Ask children to

- list a series of things that people enjoy doing during their time of rest on Shabbat. You can draw a picture of the activity or write the name of the activity.
- place the activity in the correct place on the Venn Diagram on p. 19. Would it only be done on Shabbat, done on Shabbat and at other times or only done on days other than Shabbat? There are some suggestions at the bottom of the sheet to help.

Activity 2: Shabbat guided visualisation

This guided visualisation activity is designed to help children think imaginatively about what it might be like for a Jewish person to celebrate Shabbat and to consider what a day of rest might be like in their life. Would they enjoy it? Why?

Children will need to have seen and talked about Card 10, and possibly seen one of the short BBC Learning Zone class clips referred to in Activity 1 before engaging with the guided visualisation.

Guided visualisations always begin with a stilling activity and this is included as part of the script on p.20. Some children may feel uncomfortable closing their eyes, so you could ask them to look down so that they don't disturb other children.

Ask children to

- draw, on a window outline, what they might see if they peeped into a house on Shabbat
- draw, on another window outline, what they would like to do with friends or family on a day of rest.

Activity 3: Hanukkah props bag

Show the children Card 9 and use the questions on the back to explore what is happening in the picture. Share the story of Hanukkah imaginatively with them. A clip from Sesame Street can be found at www.youtube.com/watch?v=3VfChLAADS8 .

Place a bag of props in the middle of a group of children. Ask them to decide how the festival of Hanukkah might be connected to each of the props in the bag.

The bag might include a bottle of oil, a box of eight candles, a number eight, a kippah, a wrapped present, a hanukkiah, a sword, a picture of someone praying, a doughnut box, matches, a dreidel and streamers.

Ask children to

- draw four things that they think best represent the festival of Hanukkah.

More able children can respond to the sentence starter at the bottom of the page.

Activity 4: Exploring the Ark

Share Card 11 with the children and use the questions on the back to focus on the Ark and the Torah scrolls in the synagogue.

Ask the children

- Why are these scrolls kept in a special place?
- Why are they so carefully covered and decorated?
- What things are kept really carefully in your house?

Discuss the special things that your family treasure in your house, e.g. baby photos, a pebble from a special trip, an invitation, a ticket to a special concert, a newspaper clipping.

Ask children to

- design a mantle for a Torah scroll using some appropriate colours, pictures and symbols
- design a suitable treasure box for their family and draw three things that might go in it.

More able children can label and explain the significance of the items.

Activity 1: Shabbat: Doing the delightful

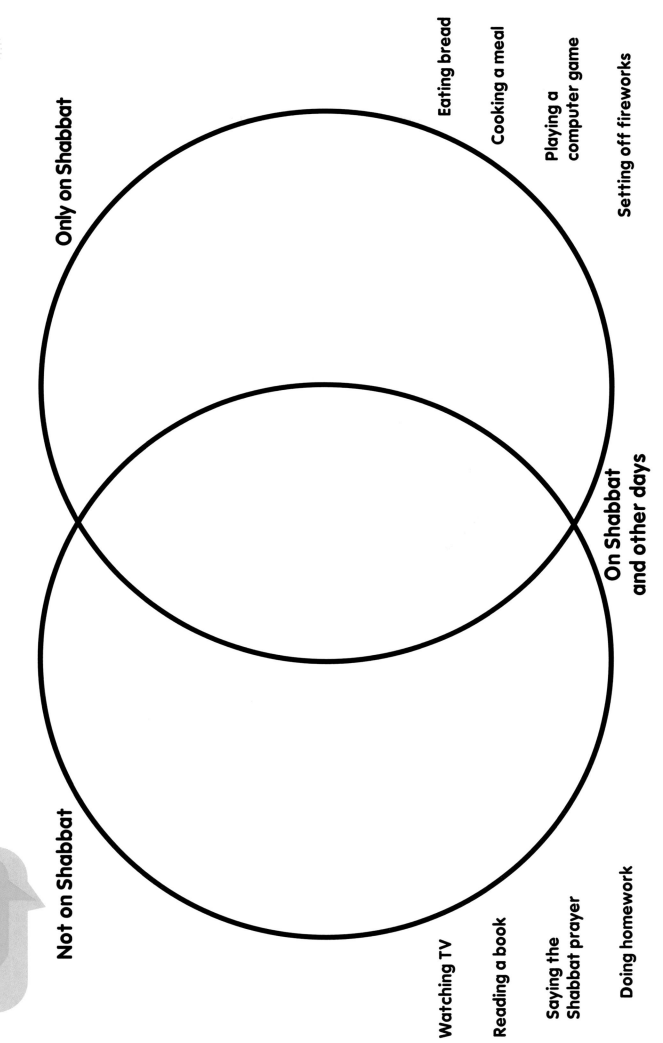

Only on Shabbat

Not on Shabbat

On Shabbat and other days

Eating bread

Cooking a meal

Playing a computer game

Setting off fireworks

Watching TV

Reading a book

Saying the Shabbat prayer

Doing homework

Activity 2: Guided visualisation: Imagining a day of rest

Preparing to imagine

- sit comfortably . . . with your back straight . . . legs crossed . . . hands in your lap . . . relaxed . . .
- let your eyes close gently . . . or look at the floor . . . so you don't disturb other people . . .
- listen to the sounds that you can hear outside the room . . .
- listen to the sounds that you can hear in the room . . .
- breathe slowly, quietly, silently . . . notice the way your breath enters and leaves your body . . .
- now listen to the scene I am going to describe to you and try and imagine it in your mind. . .

Script: Imagining a day of rest – Shabbat

You are standing in the hall of a house. It is an ordinary house a bit like the house or flat that you live in. You can hear the voices of two children, a boy and a girl. Go through the door into the sitting room . . . Look at the children . . . they are both 7 years old . . .They are finishing off some homework from school.

Look around the room. There are toys scattered around the floor . . . what can you see? The children start to clear them up into the cupboard and toy box . . . Help them to tidy up the toys . . .

The children talk about Granny and Grandpa coming round soon . . . Think about who you like to come and visit your house . . .

Dusting and hoovering are being done by Dad and the children . . . everyone is working very hard . . . but they are smiling . . .

What would you need to do in your house to prepare for a special guest?

Walk into the kitchen . . . Mum is stirring a big pan of soup on the cooker . . . it is chicken and vegetable soup . . . smell the soup . . .

From the oven Mum carefully removes a plaited challah loaf . . . it is long, with a plait down the middle . . .

Next walk into the dining room . . . here the children are setting the table . . . what can you see them putting out . . . candles . . . cups . . . a cloth to cover the bread . . . a bottle of wine . . .?

Everything is ready . . . everyone stops working hard . . . the whole family sit down together around the dining room table . . . Look at the faces of the children and the grown-ups . . . how do they feel . . .?

There is a knock at the door . . . follow the children as they run to the door. . . It is Granny and Grandpa . . . 'Shabbat shalom,' they say whilst hugging the children. . .

Everyone sits back around the table . . . Mum covers her eyes and lights the candles . . . look at the flame . . . and listen as Mum recites a blessing . . . *Blessed are you, Lord our God, King of the universe, who has made us holy through his commandments and tells us to light this Shabbat flame* . . .

It is time for everyone to eat . . . listen to the chat . . . smell the food . . .

Later . . . the whole family play a board game together in the sitting room . . . the TV isn't on . . . the computer isn't used. . . It is a time to rest from work . . . time to rest together as a family . . . no one phones up . . . nothing stops them being together.

The game is finished . . . and packed away. . .

I wonder if we peeped in later what would be happening in this house . . .?

I wonder, if there was a day of rest and delight in your house, what we would see if we peeped in through the window . . . who would be there . . . what would you do . . .?

When you are ready, open your eyes . . . quietly go to your table and draw what might happen later on Shabbat in the house we visited. . . When you have finished, quietly draw what we might see if we peeped into your house on a day of delight and resting . . .

Photocopiable by purchasing institutions

Which four props are the best reminders of Hanukkah? Draw them in the boxes below.

I think the best prop to explain Hanukkah is _____

because _____

_____

_____

My Torah mantle

My family treasure box

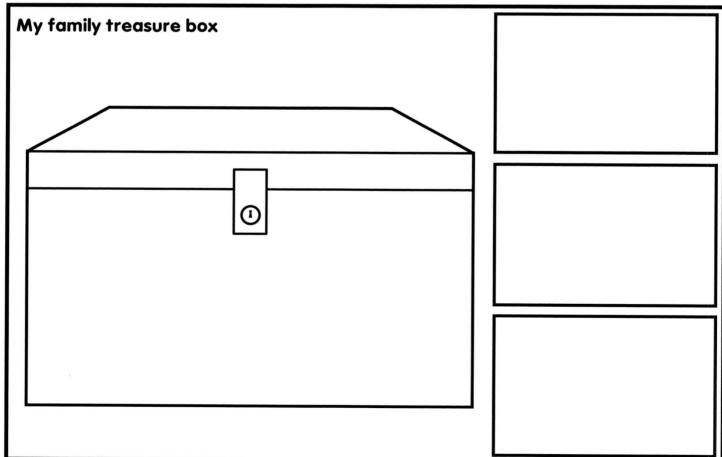

Four ways of helping lower-achieving children

Snap!

Choose four or five pictures that you want to use and reduce them on the photocopier to approximately a quarter of A4 size. Copy this sheet four times, laminate and cut them up to create a pack of simple Snap cards.

Play Snap with a pair or small group of children.

When a 'Snap' is called, the 'winner' has to point to and describe something that they can see on the photos.

You might want to make several sets of cards so that children can do the activity in small groups by themselves or with a TA.

Matching jigsaw

Cut up a copy of a picture into four, six or eight pieces, depending on the ability of the children and the detail in the picture shown.

Ask the children to remake the picture jigsaw, but as they put the pieces into place they must identify or describe or ask a question about one thing on the piece they put down.

I spy with my little eye . . .

Play the traditional game of I-Spy using a single picture or more than one picture. For children with good phonic knowledge, this game can be played using initial sound, but for other children this game can be adapted.

- *Colour I-Spy:* I spy something that is red . . .
- *Preposition and position I-Spy:* I spy something that is outside or under . . .
- *Number I-Spy:* I spy two/three . . .
- *Mood I-Spy:* I spy something happy . . .
- *Thoughtful I-Spy:* I spy something that makes me think about . . .

Dominoes

Choose eight pictures. Cut and paste them into pairs using a word processing or picture editing application. Have a mix of pairs of pictures, like dominoes. Print a pair onto A5 card, laminate them for prolonged use, and cut them up.

Give a pair of children four cards each and set it up so that they can play dominoes. They can place their card by connecting two pictures. The connection can be of any kind: for example, the child might notice that there is the same number of people in two pictures, or that there is the same colour.

After some learning using the images from elsewhere in this publication, children may be able to make a link between the same religion. At this point, the number of images chosen might be increased and more dominoes provided.

Four ways to stretch higher-achieving children

Props bag

Show the children a festival picture such as Card 9, or find other festival pictures, e.g. from the internet. Ask a group of children to investigate what the festival is about and create a props bag for it. Each prop they choose to put in the bag must have some connection, not necessarily obvious, to the festival.

A bag for Hannukah might include a bottle of oil, a box of eight candles, a number eight, a kippah, a wrapped present, a hanukkiah, a sword, and a picture of someone praying. The items can be real artefacts, or pictures.

Ask each group to join another group to present their festival props bag or present it to the class. As they reveal each item, the rest of the group or class suggest a connection to the festival.

Alternatively the festival represented could be kept secret and all the props shown at the same time. The 'audience' would then need to guess the festival before connecting each prop to it. If the 'audience' children can't guess a prop's connection to the festival, the group must reveal the connection by sharing why they chose to put it in the bag.

Tell a story

Choose some of the pictures from one faith represented in this pack. Ask children to see if they can link the pictures together and tell a story. They might do this using presentation software, dropping in pictures and adding text boxes and speech bubbles.

For example, they might write a Christmas family newsletter to be sent out with Christmas cards, telling the story of their year, imagining that all the people in the pictures are related. Starting with the Christian baptism photo, they could say that their new baby brother was born and baptised. They might choose the child in hospital and say that their brother was ill, and that lots of people prayed. Then talk about Easter, about reading the Bible, about raising money to help people in need after a disaster overseas, and ending up with Christmas.

Stories could be as simple or complex as the children can manage, but they can demonstrate how well the children have learned about and from religion.

Odd one out

Ask children to work in pairs to create an 'odd one out' challenge for another pair in the class. In order to do this they will need a copy of the blank 'odd one out' grid on p.14.

In order to create an 'odd one out' they can use one or two of the pictures from the pack but they may also want to draw a picture into a blank frame.

Children will need to be reminded that in this exercise there is no single correct answer, so each of the pictures put in the grid must be capable of being the odd one out.

Ask children creating the grid to predict the reason that someone might choose picture A, B or C as the one out. Once they have chosen their pictures and made their predictions they must give their grid to a pair of children or the whole class to try out.

Design your own Talking Pictures pack

When we put together this pack, we had to decide which parts of the RE curriculum we were going to illustrate, decide which pictures to use, write some stepped questions to go from simple to deep thinking, and write a short piece of information for teachers.

Ask children to do a version for themselves. As a class you might choose a religion and decide which areas you need to cover. You might use the 'fields of enquiry' that are commonly used in agreed syllabuses for this (i.e. beliefs, teachings and sources; practices and ways of living; ways of expressing meaning; questions of meaning, purpose and truth; questions of identity and belonging; questions of values and commitments). These 'fields of enquiry' help to make sure there are connections between learning about and learning from religion.

Ask children to produce their own cards and try them out on each other. You can then extend your own Talking Pictures pack. Send a copy to us – we'd love to see it: RE Today, 1020 Bristol Road, Selly Oak, Birmingham B29 6LB, marked 'Talking Pictures'.